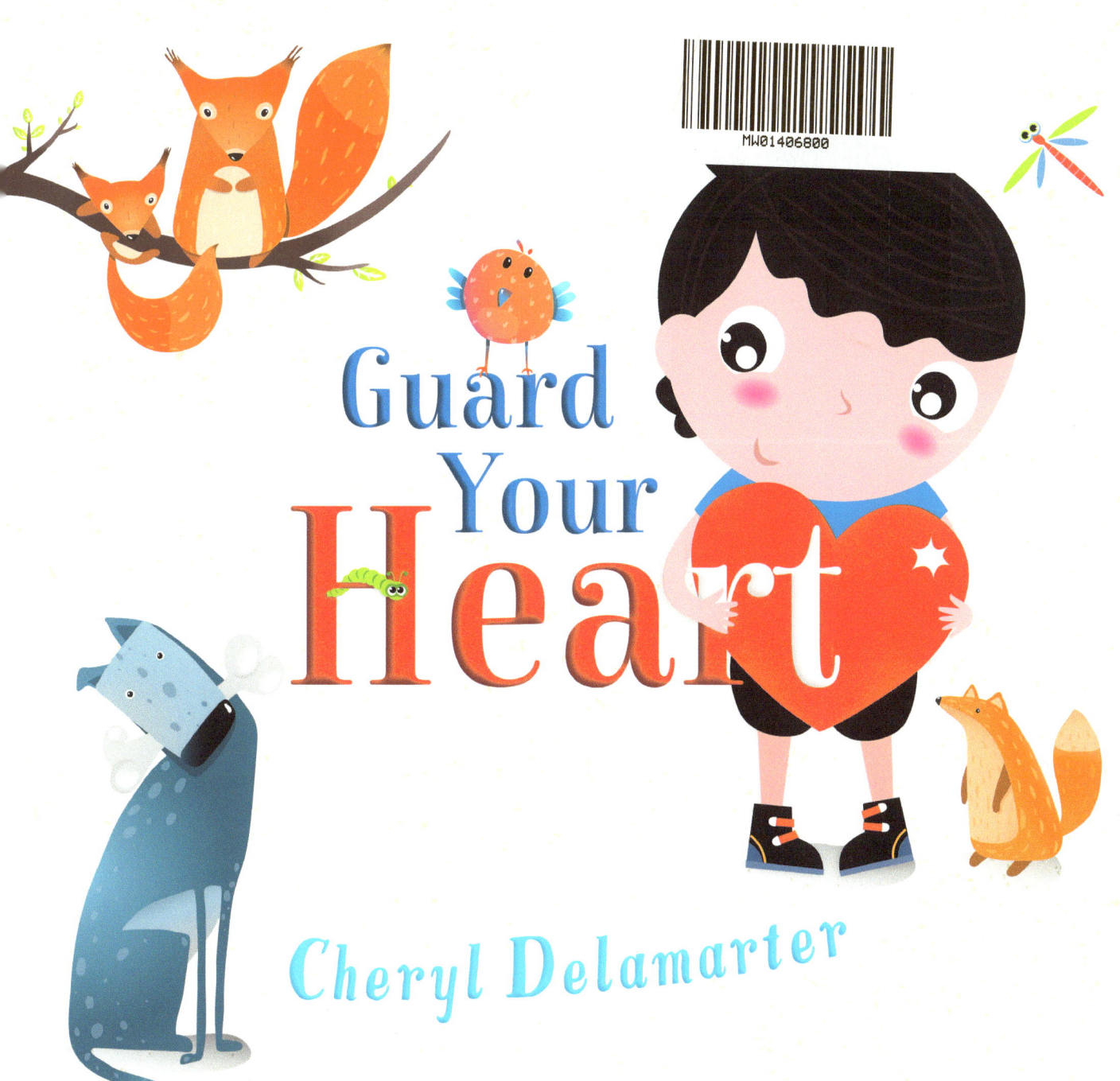

A hearty thank you to Bruce DeRoos with Left Coast Design for his amazing designs bringing life to the text of this book! Far exceeding my expectations, I am grateful for his passion for his work, his professionalism, and excellence!

A Word to Parents

The things we see, hear, witness, and experience, will shape our impressionable, moldable hearts. It is not readily noticeable, yet over time whatever it may be whether good or bad will find a place in our hearts, ultimately developing people of goodness or evil, purity or impurity with strength or weakness of character.

We must, "Test everything. Hold on to the good. Avoid every kind of evil."

I Thessalonians 5:21-22 NIV

We learn to guard our lips by the things we say, to touch a life with love, kindness, goodness, mercy, and truth.

A wise man's heart guides his mouth, and his lips promote instruction.

Proverbs 16:23 NIV

A good man out of the good treasure of his heart bringeth forth that which is good; and an evil man out of the evil treasure of his heart bringeth forth that which is evil: for of the abundance of the heart his mouth speaketh.

Luke 6:45 KJV

It is important that we teach our children to develop a discerning heart by directing them to the Scriptures, God's Holy Word; for he alone is the author of wisdom and knowledge, and in him is all truth.

> *For the Lord giveth wisdom: out of his mouth cometh knowledge and understanding.*
>
> Proverbs 2:6 KJV

As we discern what we allow our eyes to see, our ears to hear, our lives to experience, we are guarding our hearts toward what is good, holy, and right. This is the essence of life!

> *Above all else, guard your heart, for it is the wellspring of life.*
>
> Proverbs 4:23 NIV

For what we see, hear, feel, and experience will affect who we become and our response to the world we live in, to life's challenges, and to our experiences.

> *As water reflects a face, so a man's heart reflects the man.*
>
> Proverbs 27:19 NIV

Once we receive the gift of Christ's love as our Lord and Savior and daily nurture our relationship with Jesus through time in his Word, prayer, and praise, we will journey through life by the truth of the Scriptures, reflecting his beauty, his kindness, his grace and mercy toward others.

Teach me your way, O Lord, and I will walk in your truth; give me an undivided heart, that I may fear your name. I will praise you, O Lord my God, with all my heart; I will glorify your name forever. Psalm 86:11-12 NIV

Amen!

People to befriend, and

Life to experience.

Most importantly, he has given you a heart to love.

The mountains, land, and sea?

Do you choose books to read that lighten or those that darken the heart?

Do you see and ponder that which is good and pure, observing acts of love and kindness?

Or do you look upon actions that are offensive and mean?

Beware, for what your eyes see, will find a place in your heart.

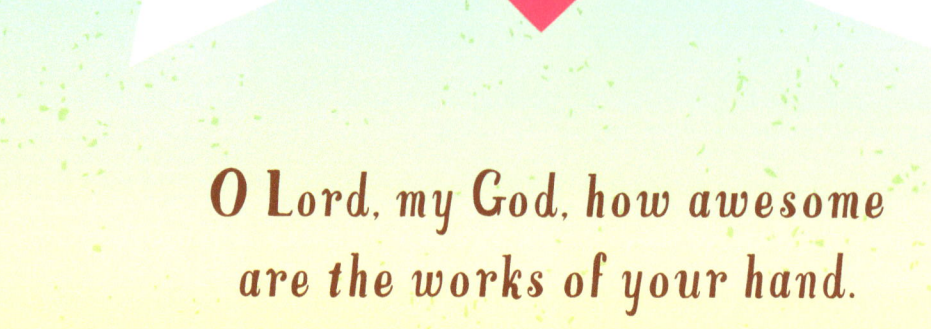

O Lord, my God, how awesome
are the works of your hand.

I AM THE WORK OF YOUR HANDS;
How I praise you for giving me life!

Help me to close my eyes from evil;
Open my eyes to all that is good.

Help me to see and rejoice in your creation,
Learn from acts of love and kindness.

Lead me by the light
of your Word, O Lord,
Create a pure heart
within me.*

In Jesus name,
I pray,
Amen

* Psalm 51:10

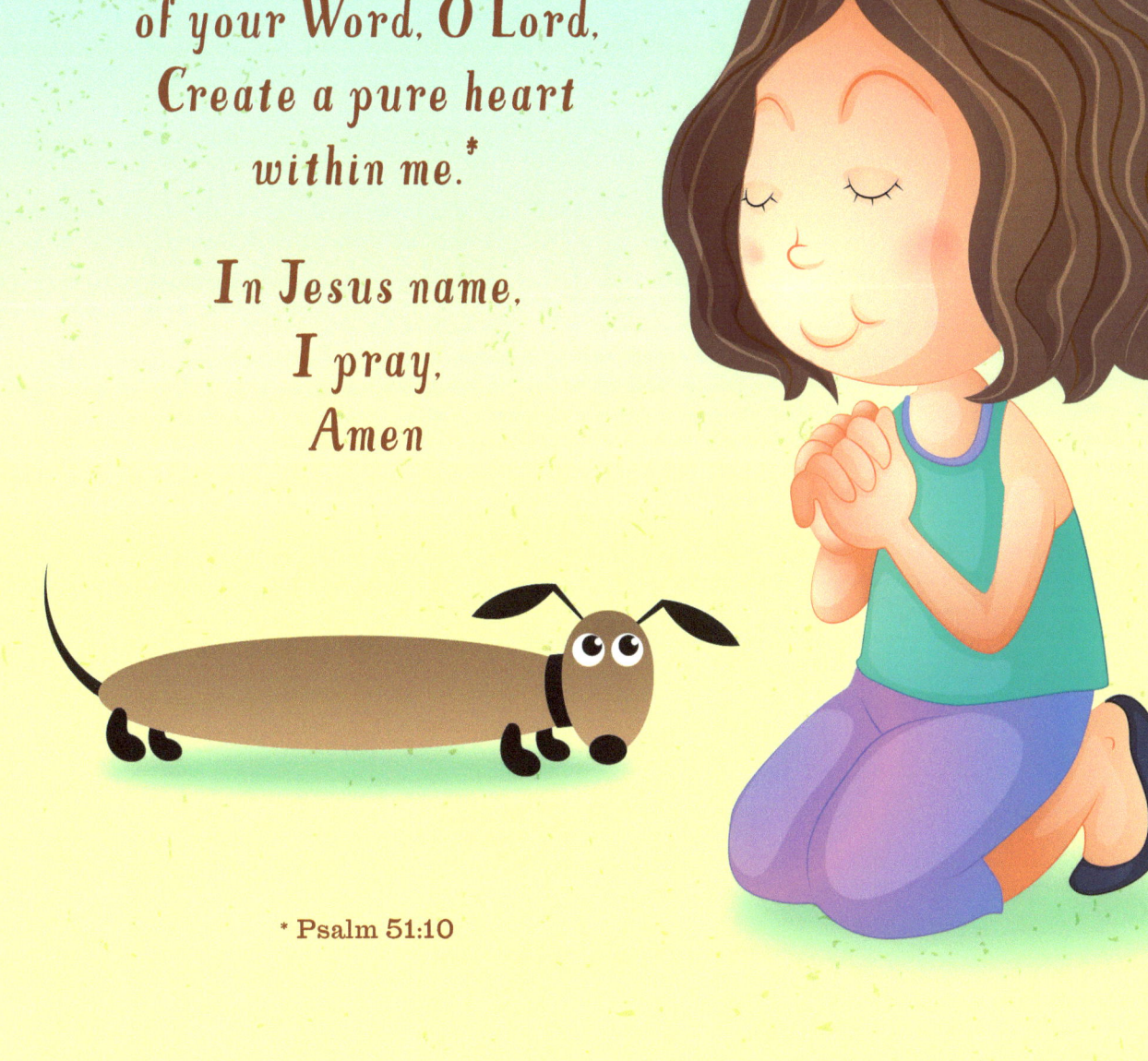

Do you pay attention to words of kindness or cruelty?

Do the words and sounds you hear bring glory or shame?

What your ears hear, WILL find a place in your heart.

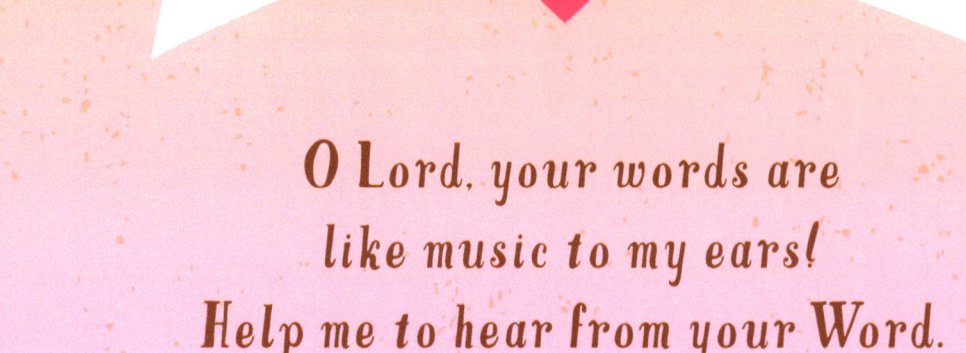

PRAYER

O Lord, your words are
like music to my ears!
Help me to hear from your Word.

Might I hear the beautiful
sounds of your creation,

The birds of the air,
The bubbling brook,
The waves of the sea,
And the sounds of the night?

OHelp me to turn away
From sounds and words
That hurt and destroy.
Please keep evil
from my heart!

Help me to listen to words
Sweet like the honeycomb*
Bringing joy and peace
to my heart;
For a heart of peace brings
Life to the body.**

In Jesus name,
Amen

* Proverbs 16:24   **Proverbs 14:30a

What type of people do you share life with?

People who speak TRUTH or lies?

People who **CARE** and **SHARE** or those who are selfish and greedy?

Choose your friends wisely; their words and actions will influence you!

Do not be misled: "Bad company corrupts good character."

I Corinthians 15:33 NIV

The people with whom you spend your time will find a place in your heart.

He who walks with wise men becomes wise, but the companion of fools will suffer harm.
Proverbs 13:20 RSV

PRAYER

O Lord, help me to love everyone,

Yet help me to be wise
in picking my friends
And those with whom I
choose to spend my time.

Draw my heart to people
who are kind and good;
May I shine your goodness
onto those who are not.

Help me to trust my parent's judgment
Regarding the people with whom I spend my time
And obey their warnings.

Thank you for giving me parents
And others to lead and guide me,
As you lead and guide them.

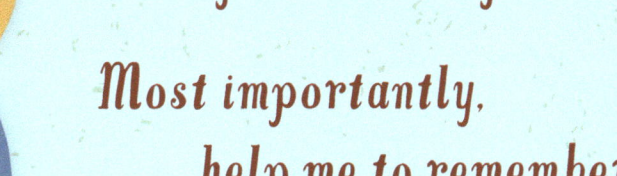

Help me to be strong
    and courageous
Doing what is right and good.

Most importantly,
    help me to remember
Love conquers all and to
    love as Jesus loves!

In His name I pray. Amen

Life experiences will mold your heart.

Disappointments and hurts, if not dealt with,

May cause bitterness to take root in your heart

Creating an angry, unhappy heart.

Anger does not bring about the righteous life God desires.*

*James 1:20 NIV

Thankfulness brings joy to the heart!
Let us praise Jesus for his goodness
and blessings to grow a happy heart.

A glad heart makes a happy face;
a broken heart crushes the spirit.
Proverbs 15:13 NLT

Emotional joys and sorrows will find a place in your heart.

A cheerful heart is a good medicine,
but a downcast spirit dries up the bones.
Proverbs 17:22 RSV

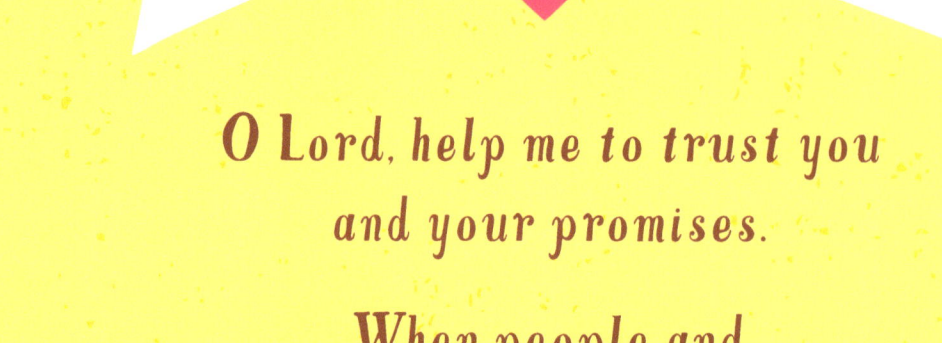

O Lord, help me to trust you
and your promises.

When people and
circumstances hurt me
And I do not understand,

I choose to trust you
To work all things for my good,
As long as I love you and live for you.*

Help me not to let anger
and bitterness into my heart.
Grow a thankful heart
within me;
I want to choose to
rejoice in all things
Because my trust is in you.**

Thank you, Jesus,
Amen

*And we know that all things
work together for good to them that
love God, to them who are the called
according to his purpose.
Romans 8:28 KJV

**Rejoice evermore. Pray without ceasing.
In every thing give thanks: for this is the
will of God in Christ Jesus concerning you.
I Thessalonians 5:16-18 KJV

Please know, the things you place in your HEART,

Through what you see,

What you hear,

What you experience, And what you feel.

Will affect the person you become.

What you hold in your heart

love

Is seen through your eyes,

Reflected on your face,

Ultimately revealed through your words and actions.

What will you place in your heart?
Who are you going to allow yourself to become?

Will your heart grow into an ugly, hardened, evil heart overflowing with brokenness and destruction?

Or, will your heart become one of beauty, reflecting love, joy, and peace???

Fill your heart every day with goodness, purity, beauty, and love according to what you see, hear, and experience. How blessed you will be!

The good man out of the good treasure of his heart brings forth what is good; and the evil man out of the evil treasure brings forth what is evil; for his mouth speaks from that which fills his heart.

Luke 6:45 NASB

Guard the words of your mouth to speak truth with kindness into others' lives.

A wise man's heart guides his mouth, and his lips promote instruction.

Proverbs 16:23 NIV

Through your words and actions, touch the heart of another to do the same.

PRAYER

May the words of my mouth
And the meditation of my heart
Be pleasing in your sight, O Lord,
My Rock and my Redeemer.*

Amen, Dear Jesus, Amen

*Psalm 19:14 NIV

Oh, that our hearts may not be tarnished by the evils around us, but remain pure just as God intends for them to be!

Blessed are the pure in heart: for they shall see God.

Matthew 5:8 KJV

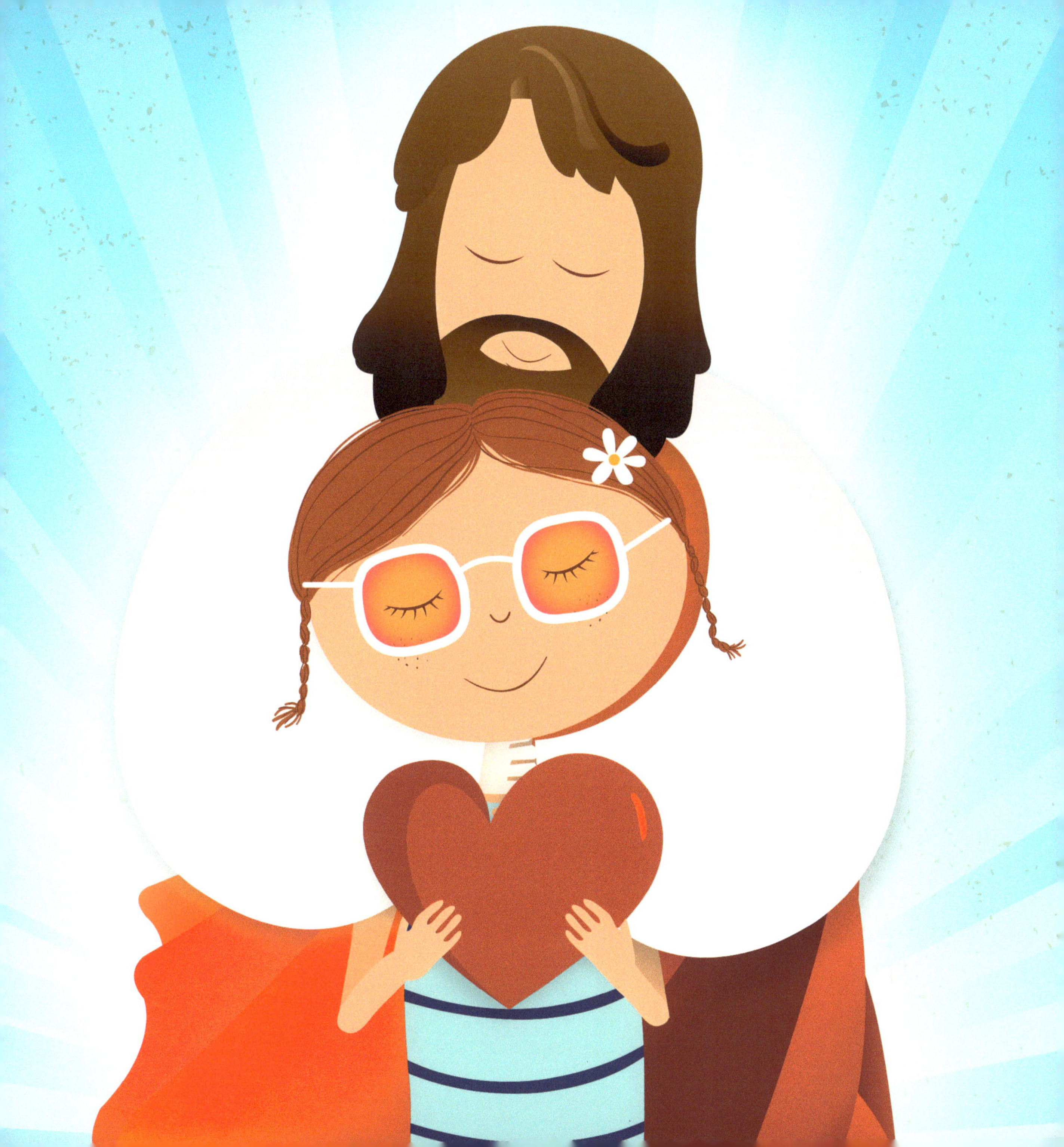

Appendix

The following Scripture verses further support the text offering words of guidance and encouragement. These may also be useful for Scripture memorization.

> Teach me your way, O Lord, and I will walk in your truth; give me an undivided heart, that I may fear your name. I will praise you, O Lord my God, with all my heart; I will glorify your name forever.
>
> Psalm 86:11-12 NIV

> ...but I want you to be wise about what is good, and innocent about what is evil.
>
> Romans 16:19b NIV

> Turn from evil and do good; then you will dwell in the land forever. For the Lord loves the just and will not forsake his faithful ones.
>
> Psalm 37:27-28 NIV

> Do not be overcome by evil, but overcome evil with good.
>
> Romans 12:21 RSV

Do not make friends with a hot-tempered man, do not associate with one easily angered, or you may learn his ways and get yourself ensnared.

Proverbs 22:24-25 NIV

Do not answer a fool according to his folly, or you will also be like him.

Proverbs 26:4 NASB

A word fitly spoken is like apples of gold in pictures of silver.

Proverbs 25:11 KJV

Incline not my heart to any evil, to busy myself with wicked deeds in company with men who work iniquity;

Psalm 141:4a RSV

For the Lord gives wisdom, and from his mouth come knowledge and understanding. He holds victory in store for the upright, he is a shield to those whose walk is blameless, for he guards the course of the just and protects the way of his faithful ones.

Proverbs 2:6-8 NIV

A heart at peace gives life to the body, but envy rots the bones.

Proverbs 14:30 NIV

For where your treasure is, there will your heart be also.

Luke 12:34 KJV

Bibliography

Life Application Study Bible,
  New International Version.
  Wheaton: Zondervan Publishing House, 2005

The Holy Bible
  King James Version by Public Domain

Revised Standard Version of the Bible
  Bible Gateway. *Web. 3 Oct. 2016*
  Revised Standard Version of the Bible, *copyright © 1946, 1952, and 1971 the Division of Christian Education of the National Council of the Churches of Christ in the United States of America. Used by permission. All rights reserved.*

New Living Translation of the Bible
  Bible Gateway. *Web. 19 Jan. 2016*
  Holy Bible. New Living Translation *copyright© 1996, 2004, 2007, 2013 by Tyndale House Foundation. Used by permission of Tyndale House Publishers Inc., Carol Stream, Illinois 60188. All rights reserved.*

New American Standard Bible
  Bible Gateway. *Web. 3 Oct. 2016*
  Copyright © 1960, 1962, 1963, 1968, 1971, 1972, 1973, 1975, 1977, 1995 by The Lockman Foundation

Illustrations

All artwork used with permission from Shutterstock.com
Cover: Copyright Jana Guothova
Copyright Popmarleo: Page 1, 2-3, 4-5, 8-9, 10-11, 19, 25, 29, 33, 34-35, 39, 43, 48, 49 52
Copyright: BlueRingMedia: Page 6-7, 12, 26
Copyright: Lorelyn Medina: Page 6-7, 13, 14, 38
Copyright: Artisticco: Page 13, 37, 46
Copyright: GraphicsRF: Page 17
Copyright: Amalga: Page 18
Copyright: Sira Anamwong: Page 18
Copyright: Stephanie Lisette: Page 20
Copyright: Oxy_gen: Page 21
Copyright: wet nose; Page 23, 31
Copyright: Katerina Davydenko: Page 24
Copyright: ayelet-keshet: : Page 27
Copyright: Aleksey Mishin: Page 28
Copyright: phlox; Page 32
Copyright: Paladjai: Page 40
Copyright: yoshi-5, Page 41
Copyright: frawcoimage: Page 44
Copyright: Jung Suk Hyun: Page 45, 47
Copyright: wizdata1: Page 49
Copyright: Amili: Page 52

FIRST SILVER THREAD PUBLISHING EDITION, OCTOBER 2016
All rights reserved. No part of this book may be reproduced, scanned, or distributed in any printed or electronic form without explicit written permission. Please do not participate in or encourage piracy of copyrighted materials in violation of the author's rights.
Silver Thread Publishing is a division of A Silver Thread, Pismo Beach, CA
www.asilverthread.com
Copyright © 2016 by Cheryl Delamarter
Cover and Interior Design by Left Coast Design, Portland, OR
ISBN 978-0-9861864-9-3
Printed in the United States of America

CPSIA information can be obtained
at www.ICGtesting.com
Printed in the USA
BVHW021805261018
531294BV00001B/21/P